SAFETY IN THE SKY

© Aladdin Books Ltd 1990

First published in 1990
in the United States by
Gloucester Press Inc
387 Park Avenue South
New York NY 10016

ISBN 0-531-17207-4
Library of Congress Catalog No: 89-81602

All rights reserved

Printed in Belgium

The front cover photograph shows planes lining up on the runway
awaiting permission to take off.
The back cover photograph shows a flight simulator of an A300 used
in pilot training.

The author, Nigel Hawkes, is diplomatic correspondent of the
Observer newspaper.

The consultant, David Learmount, is air transport editor,
Flight International.

Design: Rob Hillier, Andy Wilkinson
Editor: Margaret Fagan
Picture researcher: Cecilia Weston-Baker
Illustrator: Ron Hayward Associates

Contents

SAFETY IN THE SKY

NIGEL HAWKES

Illustrated by
Ron Hayward Associates

Gloucester Press
New York : London : Toronto : Sydney

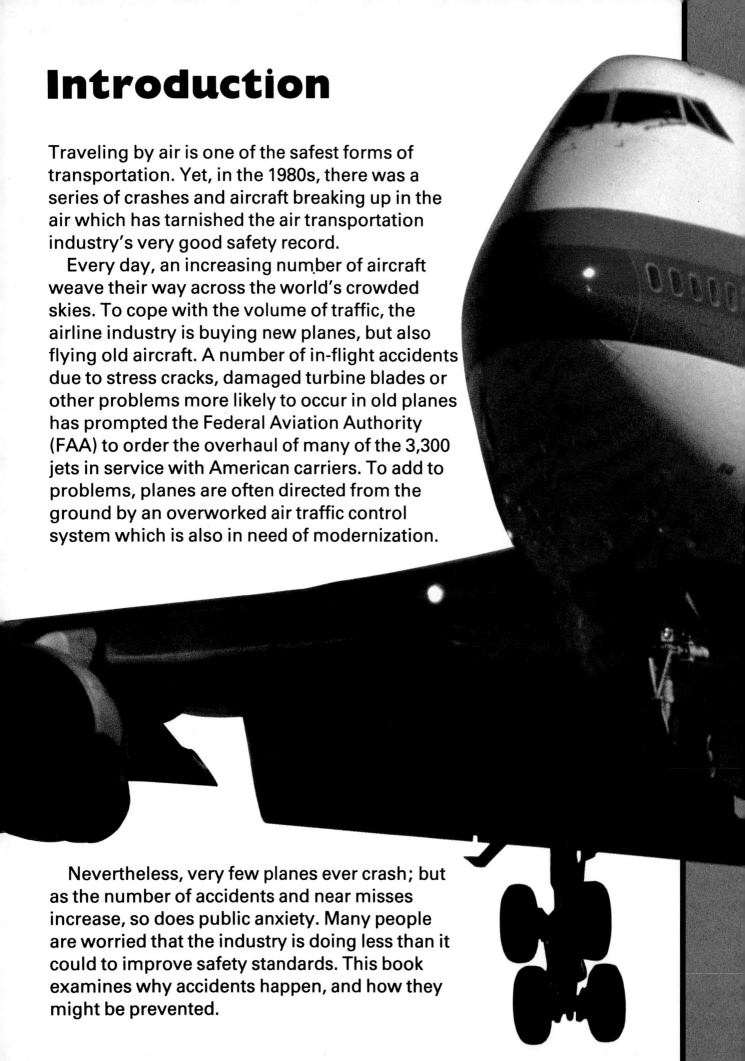

Introduction

Traveling by air is one of the safest forms of transportation. Yet, in the 1980s, there was a series of crashes and aircraft breaking up in the air which has tarnished the air transportation industry's very good safety record.

Every day, an increasing number of aircraft weave their way across the world's crowded skies. To cope with the volume of traffic, the airline industry is buying new planes, but also flying old aircraft. A number of in-flight accidents due to stress cracks, damaged turbine blades or other problems more likely to occur in old planes has prompted the Federal Aviation Authority (FAA) to order the overhaul of many of the 3,300 jets in service with American carriers. To add to problems, planes are often directed from the ground by an overworked air traffic control system which is also in need of modernization.

Nevertheless, very few planes ever crash; but as the number of accidents and near misses increase, so does public anxiety. Many people are worried that the industry is doing less than it could to improve safety standards. This book examines why accidents happen, and how they might be prevented.

A Boeing 747 jumbo jet takes off from Los Angeles international airport – just one of the thousands of aircraft in the air every day of the year to meet the insatiable demand for travel. The world's airlines have achieved extremely high safety standards, but may find it much harder to maintain these standards in the future.

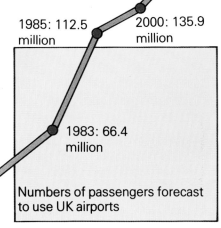

2009: 160.6 million

1985: 112.5 million

2000: 135.9 million

1983: 66.4 million

Numbers of passengers forecast to use UK airports

△ Passenger numbers in Europe are soaring, and so are the number of flights. Aircraft movements are also rising, creating serious congestion at all major airports.

The growing business

By the mid-1980s, the air transportation industry was carrying over one billion people every year, in 7,000 aircraft. The business is growing so fast that the numbers are expected to double by the beginning of the next century. Increasing prosperity means more business travel, and more people who can afford foreign vacations. In the United States, 200 million passengers are carried each year by American airlines alone – most travel on domestic routes, but numbers on long-haul flights are also increasing. The pressure on airlines is increasing and the whole system is creaking under the strain.

In the vacation months, when scheduled services share the air with charter flights, congestion becomes acute. Passengers often wait many hours before their flight can take off.

Providing enough flights has placed airline companies in a difficult situation, and their safety standards vary enormously. Some airlines use older planes, others have to "buy in" engineering skills to keep their planes safe. Good airlines are up to 40 times safer than poor ones – though no guidelines are published to tell passengers which is which. On some flights passengers are packed so tight that their chances of escape even in a minor accident are small.

In l989, the average delay at the leading British airports was 38 minutes, a 9 minute improvement on 1988. That doesn't sound too bad, but what the average really means is that while most winter flights got off on time, many peak period summer flights suffered delays of up to 12 hours.

◁ Holidaymakers bed down for a long wait. In the holiday season, when congestion is worst, some people find themselves spending the first day of their holiday in an airport terminal.

▽ On the runway, aircraft of many different airlines burn fuel to no effect as they line up in the frustrating wait for a "slot" which will enable them to take off at last.

Safety statistics

People take much greater risks every time they get into their cars or go for a walk than they do flying. Every year more people die in road accidents, at least 100 times as many as die in air crashes. Private flying in small aircraft, hot air balloons or microlights is much more dangerous than commercial flying.

Despite the headlines, flying remains one of the safest forms of travel. The number of casualties varies from year to year, from a high of more than 2,000 in 1985 to a low of 200 in 1984. But set against the great increases in air travel, the overall trend of fatal accidents is downward. The statistics can be measured in deaths per billion passenger miles. In the 1960s this figure was about three, but it has not exceeded two during the 1980s. The downward trend is mainly due to the introduction of jet aircraft which are significantly safer than older types with propellers. In 1987, for example, over a quarter of the deaths occurred in aircraft with propellers, though they accounted for only a twentieth of the total traffic.

By comparison, British figures show that railroad travel is twice as dangerous as air travel. Bus and coach travel is three times more dangerous, and car travel 25 times. The greatest risks of death come in bicycling (300 times as dangerous) and in motor-cycling (600 times). Falls in the home or the street account for 12 times as many deaths in the United States as air crashes.

▷ The map of the world is crisscrossed with the hundreds of routes occupied night and day by the 7,000-strong airline fleet.

▷ The indicator board announces flights to all over the world. Almost all will arrive safely. In 1987, a typical year, there were 25 fatal accidents on scheduled services.

南 ライウン 到着
SOUTH WING ARRIVALS

U8 50

定刻 SCHEDULED TIME	起点 FROM		航空会社 AIRLINE	便名 FLIGHT NO.	備考 REMARKS	変更/到着 WILL ARRIVE / ARRIVED
7:50	HONOLULU		PAN AM	PA3831	遅延 DELAYED	8:30
10:50	PARIS	SIBERIAN ROUTE	AIR FRANCE	AF270	遅延 DELAYED	10:55
12:00	SEOUL		KAL	KE704		
13:50		PUSAN	KAL	KE714		
13:50	SEOUL		KAL	KE7043		
14:05	FRANKFURT	POLAR ROUTE	Lufthansa	LH650		
14:20	MANILA		NORTHWEST	NW 2		
14:20	HONOLULU		PAN AM	PA831	遅延 DELAYED	14:40
14:25	SEOUL		NORTHWEST	NW 10		
14:35	NEW YORK	TRANSPACIFIC	NORTHWEST	NW 17		
14:35	TAIPEI		NORTHWEST	NW 4	遅延 DELAYED	17:00
14:35	NEW YORK		PAN AM	PA801	遅延 DELAYED	15:20
14:40	NEW YORK	TRANSPACIFIC	NORTHWEST	NW 3	遅延 DELAYED	17:30
14:45	ROME		Alitalia	AZ782		
14:50	SEOUL		KAL	KE702	機材変更 AIRCRAFT CHANGE	
15:00	HONG KONG		NORTHWEST	NW 8		
15:10	LOS ANGELES		PAN AM	PA 1	遅延 DELAYED	16:20
15:10	ZURICH		SWISSAIR	SR186	時刻変更 NEW TIME	14:45
15:10		DALLAS FORT WORTH	Thai	TG741	遅延 DELAYED	16:10
15:30	NEW YORK	TRANSPACIFIC	NORTHWEST	NW 7	遅延 DELAYED	17:15

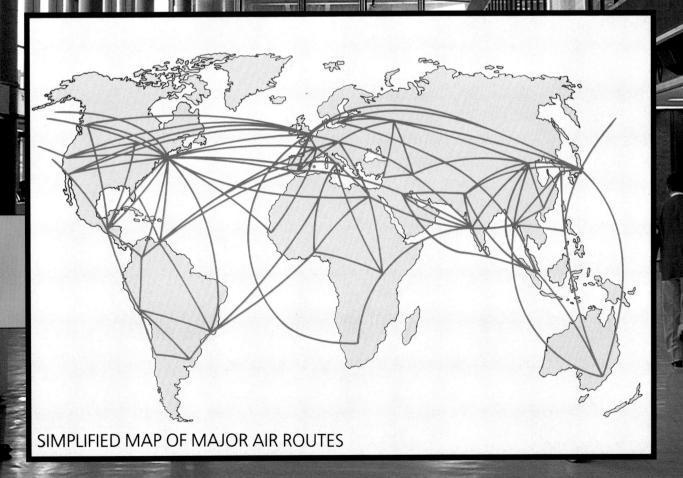

SIMPLIFIED MAP OF MAJOR AIR ROUTES

Pilot training

Two thirds of all crashes are caused by mistakes made by pilots, aircrew, or air traffic controllers. Technical failures cause 10 percent, terrorism or military action 11 percent and weather the other 12 percent. Careful design, construction and testing of new aircraft is vital; but eliminating human error has always been the single most effective way of making flying safer. Today pilots learn to fly new aircraft on flight simulators, which duplicate all the complex controls and provide an uncannily accurate impression of what it will feel like to fly the real thing.

Simulators usually cost much less than aircraft, cannot crash, and can be used to practice difficult flying conditions and to expose pilots to emergencies like engine failures, blind landings, bad weather conditions or stalls.

△ On September 4, 1989 an Ilyushin 62-M belonging to Cubana Airlines crashed just after take off from Havana. It was taking off in a thunderstorm, so it may perhaps have been hit by a sudden down-draught of air, known as "windshear," which has been blamed for 28 accidents since 1964. Pilots need to learn to cope with these difficult conditions by training on simulators. The United States Federal Aviation Administration is insisting that all airliners must have devices to warn them of windshear by 1992. The Cubana Ilyushin had no such device.

△ Pilots learn to fly the Concorde, the world's only supersonic airliner, in a simulator. They learn emergency procedures they may never need in real life.

▷ Simulators tilt and rotate to provide a convincing feeling of real flight. A view of the ground is projected onto the screen to make the illusion complete.

However, although pilots are rigorously trained, the demands of their job are strenuous. When landing, pilots may be exhausted after delays and a long flight; some have even lined up their aircraft with highways, mistaking them for the runway, until alerted by controllers. There are legal limits on the hours pilots can work, but they fly far longer than truck drivers are allowed to drive.

The legal limits designed to avoid exhaustion in pilots, allow up to 22 hours duty at a stretch. This could be made up of 9 hours on standby, 10 hours flying, and then another 3 hours at the captain's discretion.

Cabin safety

Air crashes need not kill everybody on board — investigators say that six out of ten accidents are survivable. The cabin crew have a vital part to play in any "survivable" crash and undergo intensive training to ensure they know how to deal with a cabin emergency. In August 1985 a Boeing 737 came to a halt, intact, on the runway at Manchester Airport, but 55 people died when it burst into flames. Everyone praised the heroism of the cabin crew who managed to evacuate the aircraft immediately. However, their job would have been easier, and fewer would have died, if smoke hoods and better access to the emergency exits had been available.

Airlines could also do more to provide the best safety conditions by ensuring better cabin construction; they could strengthen seat mountings or turn the seats around so that passengers face backward as they do in all military transport planes. However, no individual airline can take expensive safety measures on its own. Governments need to insist on these improvements becoming law.

▽ After an emergency landing, passengers escape by sliding down chutes. Tests show that an aircraft can be cleared in just a few minutes, but in real accidents it often takes much longer. Passengers calmly pick up their bags and duty-free goods rather than rushing for the exits.

Fire hoods are simple plastic hoods to prevent the inhalation of smoke and would improve cabin safety.

Using fireresistant materials and fitting sprinkler systems would also increase chances of survival in a fire.

Safety information from flight attendants is usually ignored.

Landing and takeoff

The most dangerous parts of a flight are takeoff and landing, when bad weather, engine failure, or pilot error can be fatal. Takeoffs with a full aircraft and a full load of fuel place maximum load on the engines, while delays on the ground can lead to icing of the wings, a frequent cause of crashes on takeoff.

Long delays on the ground have made the dangers worse, because once they have a "slot," pilots are very reluctant to turn back and lose it if an instrument indicates a minor fault. During 1989 inspectors in the United States found one aircraft flying with 55 defects awaiting repair, while another had flown for two months without an effective fuel gauge.

To ensure against defects, high standard maintenance is essential – especially in the case of older planes. The airline industry is finding it difficult to recruit enough mechanics to do the increasingly complex job of maintenance. It can require 100,000 mechanic hours for the overhaul of a single jumbo jet.

AIRPORT	DELAYED	OVER 4 HOURS
France	42	3
Yugoslavia	58	8
Portugal	58	11
*Spain	60	9
Greece	67	14
Turkey	70	16
Italy	73	11
Heathrow (UK)	34	2
Gatwick (UK)	53	7

*mainland Spain

△ Delays lead to impatience, and to the danger that minor safety warnings will be overriden or ignored. Nobody wants to go to the back of the line.

▽ Waiting for takeoff at a U.S. airport. In cold weather, wings sprayed with antifreeze can ice up during the wait.

Aircraft sometimes crash soon after takeoff because of pilot error, bad weather conditions or engine failure. In this crash, a U.S. airliner ended up in the Potomac river soon after taking off from Washington National airport. More recently, in September 1989, a U.S. Air Boeing 737 crashed into the East River in New York after trying to abort the takeoff too late. The weather was bad and the copilot, who was at the controls, had never been in the cockpit of a 737 before.In a similar accident, the crew of a Delta Air Lines Boeing 727 joked among themselves as they taxied out to take off in August 1989, forgetting to set the flaps correctly and causing a crash that killed 14 people.

Air traffic control

The crowded skies are managed by air traffic controllers, who watch the flights on radar screens and talk to pilots by radio. It is a stressful job, made no easier by out-of-date equipment.

Europe has 44 different air traffic control systems, each under national control. A decision was taken 25 years ago to set up a unified system, but it has not been carried out, and Europe's airspace remains a patchwork. A flight from Glasgow to Crete, for example, needs clearance from 10 different countries before it can even take off. Slowdowns by controllers in France and Spain, in protest against the systems they have to operate, can bring Europe's air traffic to a complete stop.

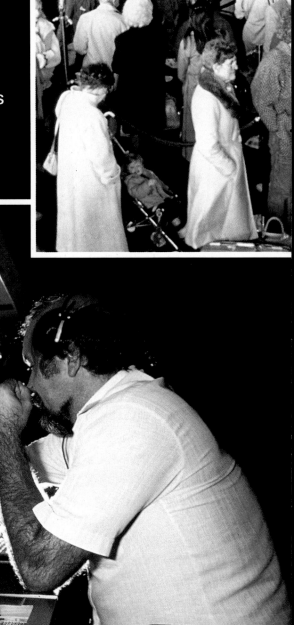

Controllers cannot give an aircraft clearance to take off until they can allocate it a "slot," and frequently have to ask it to circle in a holding pattern before it can land. In 1988 Lufthansa, the West German airline, estimated its aircraft spent 10,000 hours on the ground waiting for clearance, and 10,000 hours in holding patterns, at a total cost of $50 million.

The numbers of aircraft allowed to take off have to be limited so that the controllers are not overloaded, increasing the delays to passengers. In the sky, aircraft should fly five miles apart horizontally, and 1,000 feet vertically. But errors by pilots and controllers can lead to "air misses," when aircraft come too close and have to take evasive action. The number of air misses reported by pilots is rising, though many go unreported because pilots don't notice them in clouds, and controllers are reluctant to own up, or to blame their colleagues.

△ Deregulation of the airlines in the United States has led to more aircraft flying the same routes and trickier air traffic control. The major reason for delays in the United States, as these passengers at Boston airport are finding out, is a simple lack of runway capacity.

◁ Spanish air controllers, wrestling with what they claim are inadequate systems, have gone on strike repeatedly for more pay and additional staff. They time their strikes for busy summer weekends, when they can strand half a million vacationers.

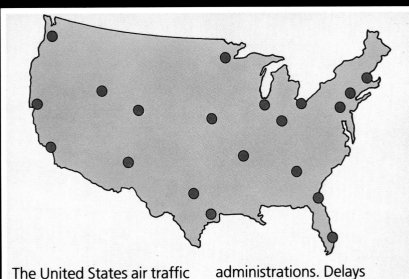

The United States air traffic control system has just 20 control centers while Europe has 44, divided among 22 different national administrations. Delays caused by a shortage of runways cost airlines in the United States an estimated $5 billion in 1989.

Accident

Even when extensive precautions are taken to ensure safety, the sad fact is that accidents still do occur.

In January 1989, 47 people died when a British Midland Airways Boeing 737 crashed on a highway near Kegworth in Leicestershire. A twin-engined aircraft, the 737 was still climbing out of Heathrow Airport en route to Belfast when an engine began to cause trouble. A fan blade had broken, causing smoke and vibration. The pilot and copilot, believing that the problem was in the right engine, switched it off, and prepared to land at a nearby airport on one engine. Tragically, they had turned off the wrong one.

▽ Firemen were rapidly on the scene of the Kegworth accident and able to pull many survivors to safety. The broken fuselage lay at the top of the highway embankment, its tail somersaulted over the rest of the plane. The closeness of the highway made it possible to get injured survivors quickly to hospitals, using procedures for dealing with major emergencies that had been practiced and worked well.

△ The "Black Box" flight recorders contain the evidence investigators need to work out the cause of many accidents. They record the setting of the throttles and controls, the airspeed, altitude and other vital details of the flight and are robust enough to survive even the most destructive of crashes.

According to international law, it is the airline which is liable for any death or injury to passengers, or loss or damage to baggage. The law is defined in the 1929 Warsaw Convention, and spelt out in the small print which nobody reads on the back of every air ticket issued.

In return for accepting this very wide definition of liability, the airlines were permitted in the convention to limit the amounts they pay out, except in cases where the victim can show that death, injury or damage resulted from the wilful misconduct of the airline's employees, which is very difficult to prove.

As they approached the airfield, the left engine failed, too late to restart the right one. The 737 crashed just half a mile short of the runway. Had the pilots made an error? Or did their instruments mislead them about which engine had failed? Careful examination of the wreckage, and the "black box" flight recorder which all airliners carry, showed clearly that the wrong engine had been turned off. But the investigators could not immediately decide why. One theory they put forward suggested pilot error could be caused by faulty instrument design.

Building new planes

Many airlines have bought new planes to carry the increasing volume of passenger traffic. But has the pressure on the manufacturers to produce new planes compromised safety? Boeing, the world's biggest plane maker, has been criticized for the design of its 747-400, with European safety officials demanding more than 30 modifications before accepting the aircraft. The most important are changes to strengthen the floor, which could cost up to £500,000 per aircraft. Boeing has also been fined $200,000 by the United States FAA for failing to report wiring problems which affected 95 of its jets. The fine is the latest of 14 imposed on Boeing since 1985 for a series of quality control failures.

△ The European Airbus is one of a new family of widebody aircraft which use only two engines. Like the twin-engined Boeing 757 and 767, the Airbus A310 and A320 are designed to be operated by a two-man crew, instead of the usual three in some aircraft. This will increase the workload on pilots, who have to do the job of the flight engineer as well as their own. In an emergency, some people fear they will be overwhelmed and unable to cope with a mass of flashing lights and alarms.

Some pilots are also anxious about the trend toward using the newly-designed twin-engined aircraft, like the Airbus or the Boeing 767, for long-haul flights across large expanses of water. Twins are more economical than four-engined aircraft, but have a smaller margin for error. But the Civil Aviation Authority and the FAA have given clearance, saying that modern engines fail only once in 30,000 hours, and the chance of losing both is one in half a billion. A twin can fly safely on one engine, right across the Atlantic if necessary.

Engine failures were once fairly common, but today's aircraft engines are so reliable that a pilot may go through his entire career without ever suffering one.

◁ The key to safety lies in the care taken on the assembly line. In recent years, the Boeing plant at Seattle has come in for heavy criticism.

Modern aircraft use lighter, stronger alloys and new materials which enable their engines to produce greater power with more reliability. But before these materials can be introduced into service, they must be tested exhaustively to ensure they have no hidden flaws that would endanger safety. Light and strong alloys also improve fuel efficiency and so cut costs.

Flying old planes

Providing enough flights for today's airline passengers has meant keeping older planes in service. Over 2,500 of the aircraft in service are more than 12 years old, and about 1,000 are flying more than 20 years after they were built. Some of these aircraft have literally begun to fall apart in the sky due to metal fatigue. In 1988 part of the fuselage of an ageing 737 broke from the plane. A stewardess was swept to her death through the hole.

The plane makers cannot keep up with demand for new aircraft. Even those airlines that can afford new planes find it hard to get them because manufacturers' order books are full. This is one reason why so many older aircraft are being kept in service.

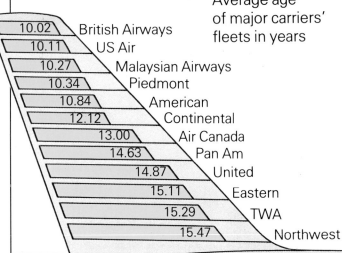

Average age of major carriers' fleets in years

Airline	Average age
British Airways	10.02
US Air	10.11
Malaysian Airways	10.27
Piedmont	10.34
American	10.84
Continental	12.12
Air Canada	13.00
Pan Am	14.63
United	14.87
Eastern	15.11
TWA	15.29
Northwest	15.47

◁ The chart shows the average age of the fleets of 12 major carriers. Airlines in the United States, which were among the first to buy the last generation of jets, are still flying them today. Many of their aircraft are 20 years old or more. But the number of flights, rather than age in years, is a better measure of how worn-out an aircraft is.

Regular inspections of in-service planes are vital, but the task of maintaining an ageing aircraft becomes increasingly inefficient as it is both expensive and time consuming. In fact, regular inspection may no longer be enough; many need to be completely rebuilt, with key parts replaced by new ones.

△ The Aloha Airlines Boeing 737, which lost its roof flying over Hawaii in April 1988, was 19 years old and had completed 89,680 flights, against a life of 75,000. Corrosion and fatigue split it open like a can of beans.

◁ If you bend a paperclip to and fro ten times or more, it will eventually break due to metal fatigue. Aircraft structures can be similarly vulnerable to countless reversals of stress and are checked rivet by rivet for possible signs of fatigue.

After the Aloha Airlines plane broke open, the U.S. authorities set up a task force to decide what to do about ageing jets. It recommended a major overhaul for 1,900 old McDonnell Douglas aircraft, and 1,300 Boeings, at a total cost of about £1 billion. U.S. airlines will need to recruit up to 50,000 new mechanics by 1997 to carry out the plans, concentrating first on aircraft that are more than 20 years old. These mechanics will also service new jets being delivered.

Sometimes hairline cracks develop behind a row of rivets due to corrosion. These can allow the aircraft to tear apart like serrated paper. Routine inspections aim to detect these faults, but sometimes fail – the crash of a Japan Airlines Boeing 747 in 1985, which killed 520 people, was blamed on this type of fault.

Terrorism

Terrorism has added an extra dimension of danger to flying in the past 20 years. A plastic bomb no bigger than a cigarette package can do enough damage to bring down a plane. Only time-consuming searches carried out before every flight can be sure of finding bombs.

On December 21, 1988, a Pan Am flight heading home for Christmas crashed over the small town of Lockerbie in Scotland. All 258 on board, and 18 on the ground lost their lives. They were victims of a bomb placed on the jet by terrorists. The motive? Revenge for the earlier downing of an Iranian airliner by missiles from an American ship, which wrongly feared it was under attack in the Gulf.

Hijacking an aircraft is another way of getting publicity for a cause. Some hijacks have lasted more than a week, with innocent passengers held hostage on the ground and sometimes cold-bloodedly killed to make a political point. Terrorists and hijackers could not flourish for long without the support of some governments: Libya, Iran, and Syria (though they protest their innocence) are the three governments most often blamed.

△ The Lockerbie bombing is thought to have been the work of a group called the Popular Front for the Liberation of Palestine (General Command), a militant terrorist organization supported by Iran. They were able to smuggle aboard the aircraft a suitcase containing a bomb made of plastic explosive. Similar bombs, built into cassette players, had been found by West German police at a flat used by members of the PLFP (GC). Yet in spite of this, and telephoned warnings received by United States embassies abroad, no special security precautions were taken.

◁ Kim Hyon Hui, a 27-year old from North Korea, was sentenced to death in 1989 for planting a bomb on a South Korean airliner and killing 115 people. Working for the North Korean Government, Kim and an older man who posed as her father left the bomb in an overhead locker. Arrested in Bahrain, the older man bit into a cyanide capsule and died. Kim tried to do the same, but was stopped. Later, she confessed to planting the bomb. The South Korean government is expected to pardon her.

In April 1988 a Kuwaiti Boeing 747 was hi-jacked by Muslim extremists, and held for more than two weeks in Cyprus and Algiers. Their aim was to secure the release of 17 fellow terrorists. The blackmail failed; but the hijackers were allowed to go free.

Airport security

Governments could do many things to make flying safer. They could get together to improve air traffic control, and insist that all airlines meet the highest standards or tell the rest of us which ones don't. They could enforce shorter hours for pilots, supply airports with the latest equipment, and refuse to accept commercial considerations as an excuse for cutting corners. But the single most effective thing they could do would be to improve security at airports, so as to prevent bombings and hijackings. It can be done, as the Israeli Government and El Al have proved for many years. But if all baggage had to be laboriously searched, it would increase delays.

Security checklist
– All baggage to be passed through scanners to detect bombs.
– Passengers should be frisked to ensure they carry no weapons.
– Passengers should identify their baggage on the tarmac to ensure that every suitcase belongs to somebody who is actually flying.
– Airport workers should be vetted for security, and airport fences guarded.

▽ Security guards at airports examine every piece of baggage with X-ray machines that can detect most bombs or weapons. Terrorists must be prevented from using passenger luggage to stow away bombs.

▽ At present, detecting bombs can be difficult. Particles detectable by X-rays should be added to plastic explosives.

An alternative might be to introduce special scents into commercial plastic explosives, so they can be detected more easily by dogs or machines. A proposal to do this is being discussed at the United Nations. More effective still would be to put pressure on the governments that protect terrorists, by isolating them diplomatically, by cutting off trade and by closing the airports of the West to their airlines. However, the problem remains of identifying the terrorists. In September 1989 a French DC-10 crashed in Niger, killing 171 people. Three different groups claimed responsibility.

Semtex

The bomb used to bring down Pan Am flight 103 over Lockerbie was almost certainly made of Semtex – a powerful plastic explosive from Czechoslovakia which can be moulded like plasticine into any shape. Semtex has no smell and does not show up on X-ray machines. A small amount of it, built into the case of a transistor radio or cassette player, will escape detection and is enough to bring down an airliner.

A machine has been made that will detect it, by bombarding baggage with particles called neutrons, and detecting the radiation given off by the explosive. Semtex, like other plastic explosives, is high in nitrogen and the gamma radiation it releases will automatically trigger an alarm. But each machine costs £500,000 so airports may be reluctant to install them.

Making flying safer

What can passengers do to ensure the best chance of a safe flight?
1. Choose an airline which is not in financial difficulties, and is based in the United States, Europe, or the more developed parts of the Far East.
2. Listen to the safety instructions, and identify the emergency exits.

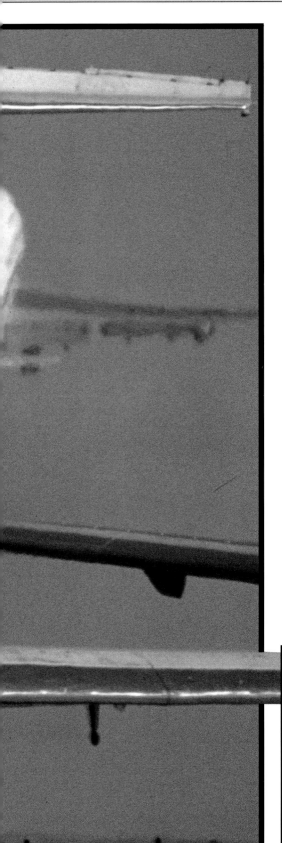

Will flying get safer in the future? The steady trend of improving safety has been shaken in the past few years. Airlines are operating in an increasingly tough commercial climate, with some losing money. Opening the market to greater competition – which has already happened in the United States, and will eventually follow in Europe – will make travel cheaper, but not necessarily safer. The chances are that the best airlines will continue to get better, while the rest, forced to cut corners to keep up, will get worse.

One problem is that every nation, however small, wants its own airline for prestige reasons. Many are unable to keep up acceptable standards. A passenger is 40 times more likely to arrive safely on an Australian airliner than on one based in Colombia. But the differences remain one of the best-kept secrets of the airline business, the result of an unwritten agreement that airlines will not compete with each other on the basis of safety. This must change. And governments must act together to ensure that all airlines are compelled to introduce further safety measures – irrespective of their financial cost.

▽ The comfortable image which airlines like to protect.

Safety facts

Chronology

1903 The first flight in a powered aircraft was made by Orville Wright on December 17, at Kittyhawk, N. Carolina. It lasted 12 seconds.

1908 The first passenger flight took place, also at Kittyhawk, when Wilbur Wright took his mechanic, Charles Furnas, aloft for 29 seconds. On September 17, the first person

Airport safety

At least ten of the world's airports are "critically deficient," according to the International Federation of Airline Pilots' Associations. The map below shows the most dangerous airports.

to be killed in an accident in a powered aircraft was Lt Thomas Selfridge, of the U.S. Army Signals Corps, when a biplane flown by Orville Wright, in which Selfridge was a passenger, crashed.

1914 Scheduled services by air were begun by the St Petersburg-Tampa Airboat Line, flying passengers one by one across Tampa Bay in a Benoist flying boat.

1919 International airline services began between Paris and Brussels, operated by Lignes Aerienne Farman, on March 22. On August 25, the first international flights on a daily schedule began between London and Paris.

1920 The first disaster on a scheduled passenger flight killed the two-man crew and two passengers when an aircraft belonging to Handley-Page Continental Air Services crashed into a house in a London suburb shortly after takeoff.

1922 The first collision between airliners took place on April 22, when a Farman Goliath collided with a Daimler DH 18 over northern France.

1930 Ellen Church, the first air hostess, began work on May 15 on a United Airlines flight between Oakland, California, and Cheyenne, Wyoming. Air France recruited its first air hostesses the following year.

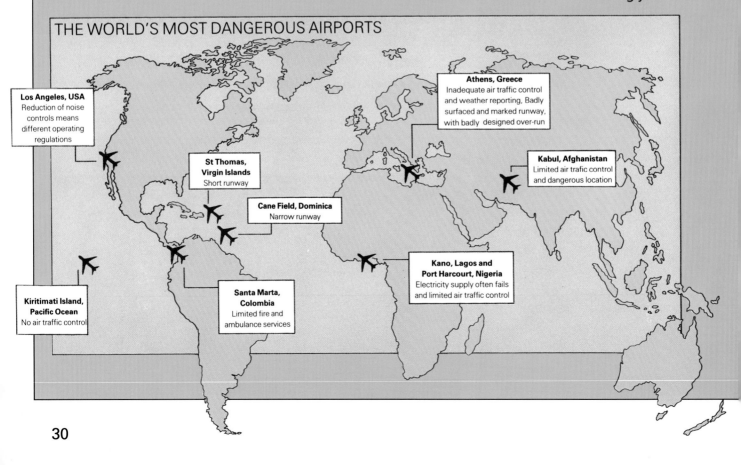

THE WORLD'S MOST DANGEROUS AIRPORTS

Los Angeles, USA
Reduction of noise controls means different operating regulations

Athens, Greece
Inadequate air traffic control and weather reporting, Badly surfaced and marked runway, with badly designed over-run

Kabul, Afghanistan
Limited air trafic control and dangerous location

St Thomas, Virgin Islands
Short runway

Cane Field, Dominica
Narrow runway

Kano, Lagos and Port Harcourt, Nigeria
Electricity supply often fails and limited air traffic control

Kiritimati Island, Pacific Ocean
No air traffic control

Santa Marta, Colombia
Limited fire and ambulance services

1939 The first scheduled transatlantic flights were started by Pan American, flying Boeing flying boats between Newfoundland and Southampton. Each passenger had a separate cabin, there was a recreation lounge, a dining saloon and a bridal suite. The fare was £140 return and the flight took almost 19 hours.

1948 The world's first aircraft hijack took place when Cathay Pacific's Catalina flying boat *Miss Macao* was taken over by a gang of bandits led by Wong yu Man on a flight between Macao and Hong Kong. The gang wanted to ransom the passengers, but when the pilot resisted they fired their guns, bringing the aircraft down. Wong yu Man was the sole survivor.

1955 On November 1, a Douglas DC-6B of United Air Lines was blown up in flight near Longmont, Colorado, by a bomb placed by John Graham in order to murder his mother, who was on the flight, and claim her life insurance.

1974 The greatest number of passengers ever carried on a single flight was 674 (306 adults, 328 children and 40 babies) on a Boeing 747. The passengers were being evacuated from Darwin, which had been hit by a cyclone, to Sydney, on 29 December.

1977 The worst crash in the history of aviation occurred on the ground in Tenerife on March 27, when two Boeing 747s, one from KLM and the other from Pan Am, collided with the loss of 583 lives.

1989 In July Alfred Haynes brought down a crippled United Airlines DC-10 into Sioux City without hydraulic power, saving 187 of his passengers. Haynes had only the engines to control the aircraft. Haynes almost made it, but 100 yards short of the runway the right wing dipped, and without controls he could not correct it. The plane crashed and 110 died – but Haynes, his crew, and 183 passengers survived.

1989 In September a Boeing 737 of Varig Airlines took off from Sao Paulo for Belem – and flew off in entirely the wrong direction. When it ran out of fuel over the Amazon jungle, the pilot was forced to make a "delicate" landing on the tops of the trees. The aircraft broke up, but amazingly 42 out of the 54 aboard survived, to be rescued four days later suffering from thirst, bee stings and insect bites.

Air Traffic Control

The chaos of European air traffic control systems could be ended by a new company, jointly owned by the airlines and national governments, which would take over control. The plan comes from 21 European airlines frustrated by delays which cost them £3 billion a year.

The airlines launched their plan in September 1989, and say it should be possible to get it into operation by 1991. Europe spends as much every year to control aircraft movements as the United States ($1.6 billion), even though there are only a third as many aircraft movements in Europe. However hard governments try to make the existing system work, it simply does not have the capacity.

While some parts of the system could handle many more aircraft, the system as a whole has to work at the speed of its slowest members. To put this right will involve investment, and cutting the existing 44 control centers down to perhaps six. The airlines' plan is revolutionary because it would involve taking away control of airspace from national governments and putting it in the hands of the new company. For that reason, many people doubt that European governments will be willing to accept it.

Index